Little Mitchie

DO FISH SLEEP?

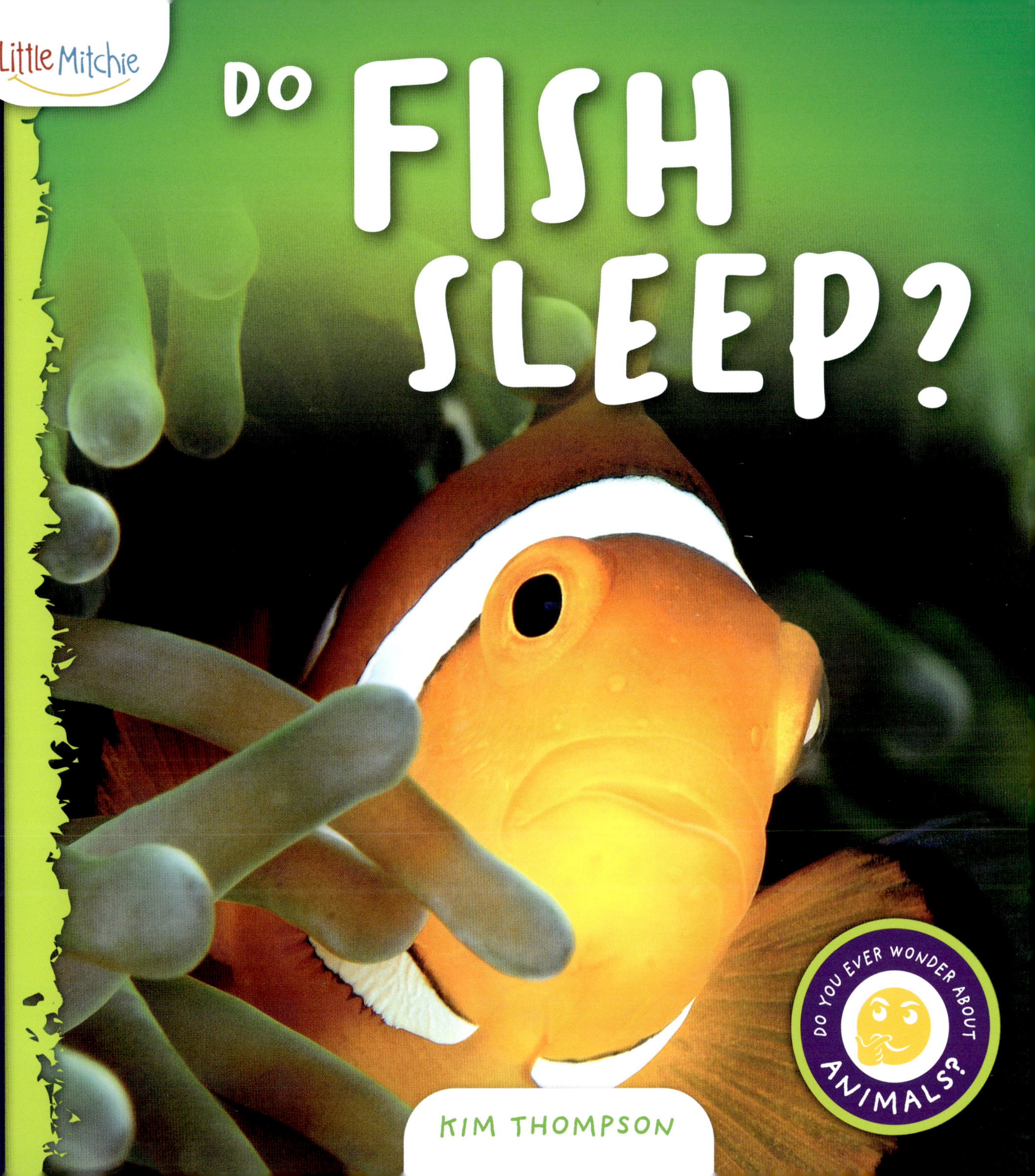

DO YOU EVER WONDER ABOUT ANIMALS?

KIM THOMPSON

CREATING YOUNG NONFICTION READERS

Little Mitchie books spark curiosity and support early nonfiction reading for students in Grades 2-3. Designed to build vocabulary, support second language learners, and prepare readers for middle-grade content, each book includes helpful tips for parents and educators to build confidence and deepen understanding of the world.

TIPS FOR READING NONFICTION WITH BEGINNING READERS

Talk about Nonfiction

Begin by explaining that nonfiction books give us information that is true. The book will be organized around a specific topic or idea, and we may learn new facts through reading.

Look at the Parts

Most nonfiction books have helpful features. Our *Little Mitchie* titles include color photographs and graphic aids, a table of contents, a glossary, and an index. Share the purpose of these features with your reader.

Color Photos and Graphic Aids

A lot of information can be found by "reading" photos, charts, maps, and other graphic aids found within nonfiction texts. Help your reader learn more about the different ways information can be displayed.

Table of Contents

Located at the front of the book, this list shows the big ideas within the text and the page numbers where they can be found.

Glossary

Located at the back of the book, the glossary defines key words and phrases that are related to the topic. These words and phrases can be found in the text in colored type.

Index

Located at the back of the book, an index is an alphabetical list of topics and the page numbers where they can be found.

With a little help and guidance about reading nonfiction, you can feel good about introducing a young reader to the world of *Little Mitchie* nonfiction books.

Little Mitchie is an imprint of:

Mitchell Lane
PUBLISHERS

2001 SW 31st Avenue
Hallandale, FL 33009
mitchelllanepub.com

First Edition, 2027.

Author: Kim Thompson
Designer: Jen Bowers

Library of Congress Cataloging-in-Publication Data
Title: Do Fish Sleep? / by Kim Thompson

Description: Hallandale, FL :
Mitchell Lane Publishers, [2027]

Identifiers:
ISBN 979-8-89260-922-7 (library bound)
ISBN 979-8-89260-977-7 (eBook)

Library of Congress Control Number: 2026935236

PHOTO CREDITS
Shutterstock: cover, p.1 ©2017 Subphoto.com, p.5 ©2019 Simon Shin kwangsig, p.6–7 ©2017 Rich Carey, p.9 ©2012 Guido Montaldo, p.10–11 ©2017 David A Litman, p.13 ©2020 BlueRushDepth, p.14 ©2025 lilit01, p.17 ©2015 Kletr, p.18–19 ©2017 wildestanimal, p.21 ©2021 Kurit afshen, p.22 ©Liu Boyuan

TABLE OF CONTENTS

Chapter One

QUESTIONS

Have you ever watched fish? Did you see them darting around or swimming together in a **school**?

You probably wondered about these **aquatic** animals. You may have asked these questions.

1. How do fish swim?
2. Why do fish swim?
3. Do fish ever sleep?

Chapter Two

SWIMMING LIKE A FISH

Fish swim by moving their bodies and tails from side to side. **Fins** help them balance, steer, and slow down.

ANIMAL WONDER

Not all water animals are fish. A fish has a backbone. It is **cold-blooded**. It breathes through **gills**.

Some fish swim around constantly. Others do not go far. They may stay near the bottom of oceans, lakes, ponds, and rivers.

ANIMAL WONDER

Schools of fish swim together in the same direction. They keep an equal amount of space between each fish.

Chapter Three

SWIMMING TO LIVE

Fish swim to find food. They swim to escape from enemies.

Some fish are active during the day. Others swim more at night. Some fish live in the depths of the ocean. They may not know if it is day or night.

ANIMAL WONDER

Some fish use a shortcut. They hang out in **currents** that move water through their gills.

Many fish must swim in order to breathe. Swimming makes water flow through their gills. The gills take **oxygen** out of the water.

Some fish can breathe without swimming. They move their jaws to make water pump through their gills.

Chapter Four

SLEEP-SWIMMING

Even swimming fish need rest. Their brains need a chance to recharge.

ANIMAL WONDER

Most fish don't have eyelids. Sharks are some of the only fish that can close their eyes.

Scientists study fish **behavior**. They think most fish spend time in a resting, sleep-like state.

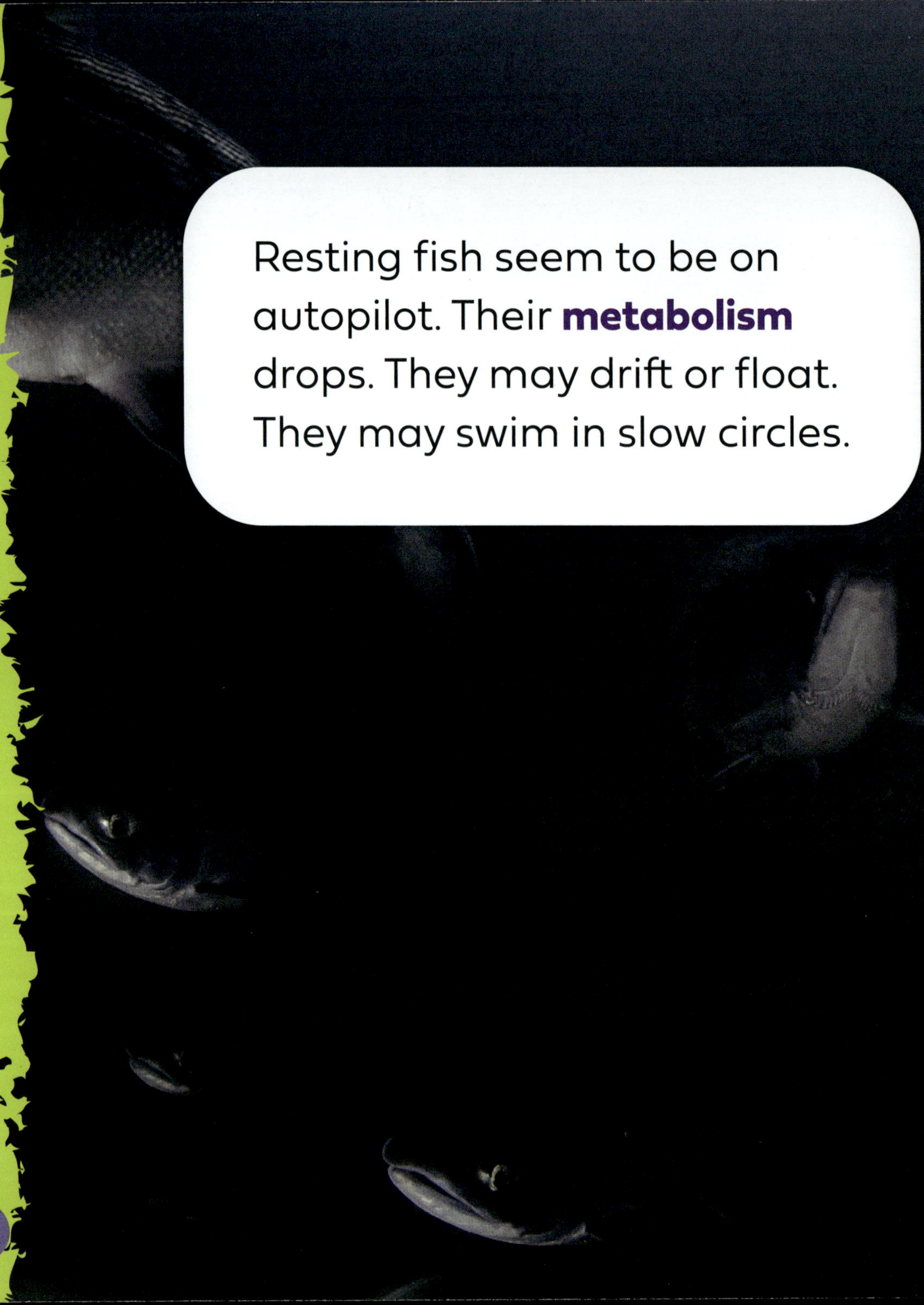

Resting fish seem to be on autopilot. Their **metabolism** drops. They may drift or float. They may swim in slow circles.

ANIMAL WONDER

Fish may use **unihemispheric** sleep. That means one side of the brain is awake while the other half sleeps.

Chapter Five

ANSWERS

Now, you can answer your questions.

1. **HOW DO FISH SWIM?**

   Fish move special body parts to travel through the water alone or in schools.

2. **WHY DO FISH SWIM?**

   Fish swim to find food, escape enemies, and keep water pumping through their gills so they can breathe.

3. **DO FISH EVER SLEEP?**

   Fish keep swimming as they enter a resting, sleep-like state.

ANIMAL WONDER

Keep asking questions about animals. That's how you learn about the amazing creatures that share our world!

FISH DIAGRAM

GLOSSARY

aquatic (uh-KWAH-tik) living or growing in water

behavior (bi-HAYV-yur) the way an animal acts

cold-blooded (kohld BLUHD-id) unable to make body heat; having a body temperature that changes with the temperature of the surroundings

currents (KUR-uhnts) movements of water in a definite direction in a river or ocean

fins (finz) flap-shaped body parts that fish use to move and steer through the water

gills (gilz) organs near the mouth that fish use to breathe underwater

metabolism (muh-TAB-uh-liz-uhm) the process by which food is changed into energy; digestion

oxygen (AHK-si-juhn) a gas with no color that animals need to breathe

school (skool) a group of fish that swim and feed together

unihemispheric (yoo-nuh-hem-uh-SFEER-ik) relating only to one side of a two-sided object, such as an animal's brain

FURTHER READING

Kurtz, Kevin. *A Junior Scientist's Guide to Diverse Habitats, Colorful Species, and Life Underwater.* Callisto Kids, 2021.

Shumaker, Debra Kempf. *Freaky, Funky Fish: Odd Facts about Fascinating Fish.* Running Press Kids, 2021.

ON THE INTERNET

Fun Kids Live: Top 10 Facts about Fish!
funkidslive.com/learn/top-10-facts/top-10-facts-about-fish
Learn fascinating fish facts.

Nat Geo Animals: How Do Fish Sleep?
youtube.com/watch?v=-N15GyYRy7c
Go on a dive to sneak up on catfish taking a nap.

San Diego Zoo Kids: Do Fish Sleep?
youtube.com/watch?v=WLqowGFNgzs
Watch an expert explain how to tell if a fish is sleeping.

INDEX